STEM ADVENTURES

TERRIFIC
TECHNOLOGY

D1542401

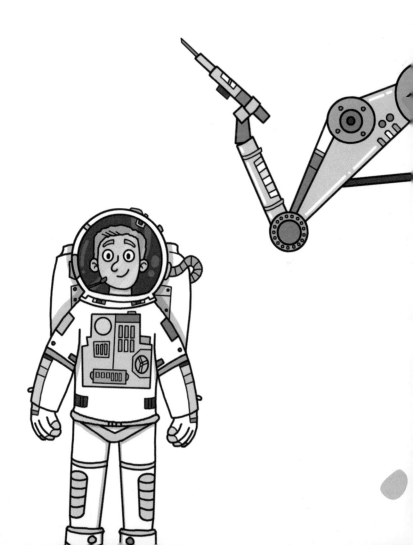

First edition for the United States
and Canada published in 2018
by Barron's Educational Series, Inc.

All inquiries should be addressed to:
Barron's Educational Series, Inc.
250 Wireless Boulevard
Hauppauge, NY 11788
www.barronseduc.com

ISBN: 978-1-4380-1252-0

Date of Manufacture: July 2018
Manufactured by: RRD Asia, Dongguan, China

Printed in China
9 8 7 6 5 4 3 2 1

Executive editor: Bryony Davies
Design: Kate Wiliwinska
Designed and packaged by: The Shop
Illustrated by: Dynamo Limited
Picture research: Steve Behan and Paul Langan
Production: Nicola Davey

AUTHOR:

CLAIRE SIPI worked in the children's publishing
industry for more than 25 years, specializing in licensed
publishing and nonfiction reference titles, ranging from
first encyclopedias to books on dinosaurs, nature,
animals, science, technology, and gadgets.

STEM EDITORIAL CONSULTANT:
MARGARET (MEG) KÄUFER is a
founding member and current president of the STEM
Alliance of Larchmont-Mamaroneck, NY. The STEM
Alliance is a nonprofit organization with the mission of
creating a network of STEM learning opportunities to
connect today's youth to the jobs of the future. They work
closely with local schools to run hands-on, applied STEM
enrichment experiences. Highlights of their work under
her leadership include launching an annual public STEM
festival, establishing competitive robotics teams, and
creating a hands-on STEM summer enrichment program
for at-risk children. Meg has her Masters in Curriculum &
Instruction from Teachers College, Columbia University.
Throughout her career, Meg has championed STEM
learning for its capacity to engage and inspire all
varieties of learners.

PICTURE ACKNOWLEDGMENTS
The publishers would like to thank the following sources for their kind
permission to reproduce the pictures in the book.

Pages 6–7: Alexandr III/Shutterstock; 9 (top right): Olas/Shutterstock,
(bottom): Bsd/Shutterstock; 10 (bottom left): Odili/Shutterstock; 11 (top):
Ntkris/Shutterstock, (bottom): Vladislav Gajic/Shutterstock; 12 (top right):
Ljupco Smokovski/Shutterstock, (bottom left): Giorgiomtb/Shutterstock;
13 (top right): Pavle Marjanovic/Shutterstock; 14 (top left): Monticello/
Shutterstock, (top center): TanyaRozhnovskaya/Shutterstock, (top
right): Science History Institute/Wikimedia Commons, (bottom left): Photo
one/Shutterstock, (bottom center): Anelina/Shutterstock, (bottom right):
DenisNata/Shutterstock; 16 (top right): Maggee/Shutterstock; 17 (top
right): De Visu/Shutterstock; 18 (top right): Public Domain; 21 (top right):
Osugi/Shutterstock; 23 (top): Mr. Khatawut/Shutterstock; 25 (bottom
right): Psgxxx/Shutterstock; 26 (top right): Aleks Melnik/Shutterstock; 27
(top center): Irin-k/Shutterstock, (top right): Duda Vasilii/Shutterstock,
(bottom): Mascha Tace/Shutterstock; 28 (bottom left): Muratart/
Shutterstock; 29 (top left): Dmitry Kalinovsky/Shutterstock, (bottom left):
AboutLife/Shutterstock; 30 (top right): DRogatnev/Shutterstock, (bottom
right): Innershadows Photography/Shutterstock; 31 (bottom right): Private
Collection; 32 (bottom left): Zapp2Photo/Shutterstock; 33 (top right):
Sportpoint/Shutterstock; 35 (bottom right): KaliAntye/Shutterstock; 37
(left): D.Kucharski K. Kucharska/Shutterstock, (right): Waj/Shutterstock,
(bottom left): Bluecrayola/Shutterstock, (bottom right): Plenoy m/
Shutterstock; 39 (top): Winui/Shutterstock; 40 (bottom right): Public
Domain; 42 (bottom left): Twin Design/Shutterstock; 44 (top left): Bart
Sadowski/Shutterstock; 45 (bottom): Vlad Kochelaevskiy/Shutterstock;
46 (top right): Library of Congress, (bottom right): Svetlana Zhukova/
Shutterstock; 49 (top left): Anan Kaewkhammul/Shutterstock, (top
right): Dena17/Shutterstock, (left): Anton_novik/Shutterstock, (right):
kc_film/Shutterstock; 50 (top right): 3Dsculptor/Shutterstock; 52 (top
right): ALPA PROD/Shutterstock; 53 (bottom left): Phoniamal Photo/
Shutterstock; 54 (center): S.Bachstroem/Shutterstock, (bottom left):
Chatchawal Kittirojana/Shutterstock; 58 (left): JPL/NASA, (right): Andrey
Armyagov/Shutterstock, (bottom left): NASA, (bottom right): NASA; 60
(top right): Rawpixel.com/Shutterstock, (bottom): RozKa/Shutterstock;
61 (bottom): Mascha Tace/Shutterstock

Every effort has been made to acknowledge correctly and
contact the source and/or copyright holder of each picture,
and Carlton Books apologizes for any unintentional
errors or omissions, which will be corrected in
future editions of this book.

STEM ADVENTURES

TERRIFIC
TECHNOLOGY

Claire Sipi

BARRON'S

CONTENTS

SUPER STEM

Welcome to the world of STEM. STEM stands for science, technology, engineering, and math. These four fabulous subjects open up a world of exciting discovery.

You probably already possess many of the qualities and interests shared by great scientists, technologists, engineers, and mathematicians. Read each statement and put a check in the box if it applies to you.

SCIENCE

YOU...

- are curious about the world around you. ☐

- love to ask questions. ☐

- experiment and try new things, even if it means making a mistake. ☐

You're already on your way to becoming a scientist! You're excited to discover more about the way scientists think and work.

TECHNOLOGY

YOU...

- are always playing with gadgets. ☐

- like to understand exactly how machines work. ☐

- try to find ways of making everyday tasks easier, such as investigating whether a different route to school makes the trip shorter. ☐

Technology is right up your alley! You're fascinated by the latest products and want to find out more about inventions that help improve our world.

ENGINEERING

YOU...

- like using your brain to solve problems. ❑

- love playing with construction sets and building blocks. ❑

- enjoy building amazing dens or dams in streams. ❑

You're perfectly suited to a career as an engineer! You could invent or make amazing tools, machines, and buildings.

MATH

YOU...

- like to understand the reasons why something is true. ❑

- often spot patterns in pictures and clothing or sequences in numbers like football statistics. ❑

- love 3-D puzzles, card games, and logic games like chess. ❑

You're a born mathematician! You're excited by shapes and measurements and curious to see what numbers can do when you use them in different ways.

WHAT IS TECHNOLOGY?

This book is all about technology, which helps humans succeed in their environments. If you love problem solving, making and designing things, thinking BIG, and, of course, gadgets, robots, and machines, then you already have what it takes to work in this fascinating field!

In technology, people use their knowledge of the world to invent and develop products that will improve our day-to-day lives. It's not just about state-of-the-art computers, though. Engines, books, and tools are all super-useful examples of technology that is used across the globe. Technology is filled with amazing ideas and inventions—in fact, we'd be lost without it!

IN THE BEGINNING...

Technology began about 2.5 million years ago when our ancestors first started making stone tools for hunting, building, and eating. As these early humans developed, their tool-making skills improved with the use of bones, wood, and eventually metal. These tools helped them farm, cook, build, hunt, and make clothes.

ACTIVITY

Look at all these ancient tools. Can you match each one up to its modern name? If you aren't sure, take a guess!

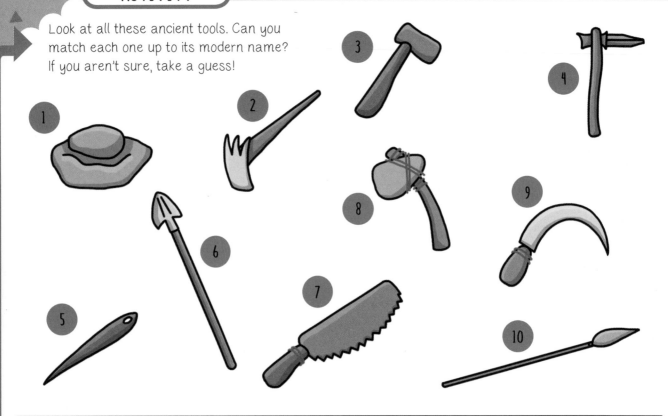

SAW

SPEAR

SICKLE

AXE

HAMMER

HOE

ARROW

CHISEL

NEEDLE

PESTLE AND MORTAR

CHECK THE ANSWERS AT THE BACK OF THE BOOK!

A tool does its job by using force—the push or pull on an object. Tools get force from the kinetic energy you make when you bang, push, pull, or turn the tool.

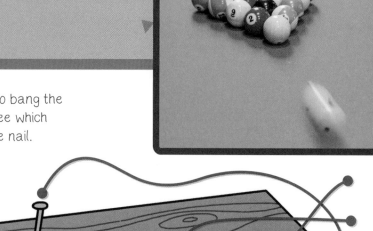

Kinetic energy is the energy an object has due to its motion.

ACTIVITY

Which hammer is the carpenter using to bang the nail into the wood? Follow the trail to see which tool will connect its kinetic energy to the nail.

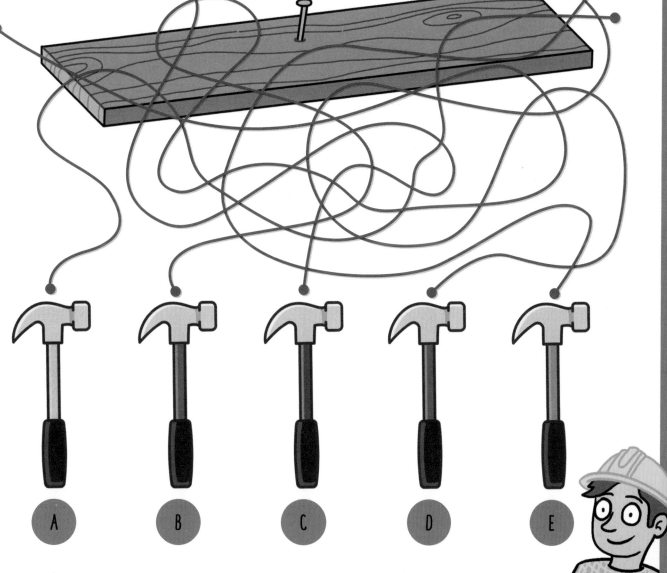

A   B   C   D   E

CHECK THE ANSWERS AT THE BACK OF THE BOOK!

MARVELOUS MACHINES

A machine makes a job easier to do. Machines have moving parts, called mechanisms, that change the direction of the force being used or multiply the force being applied to it. The most commonly used and simplest mechanisms are levers, pulleys, wheels, and gears.

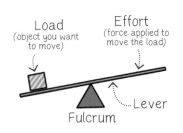

LEVERS

A lever is a rigid bar that tilts at a point called a pivot or fulcrum. The fulcrum can be moved to decrease the amount of effort needed to lift the load.

Load
(object you want to move)

Effort
(force applied to move the load)

Lever

Fulcrum

ACTIVITY

A seesaw is a type of lever. To balance the seesaw, each end of the lever has to have the same load (weight) on it. Balance these seesaws by adding on the correct loads.

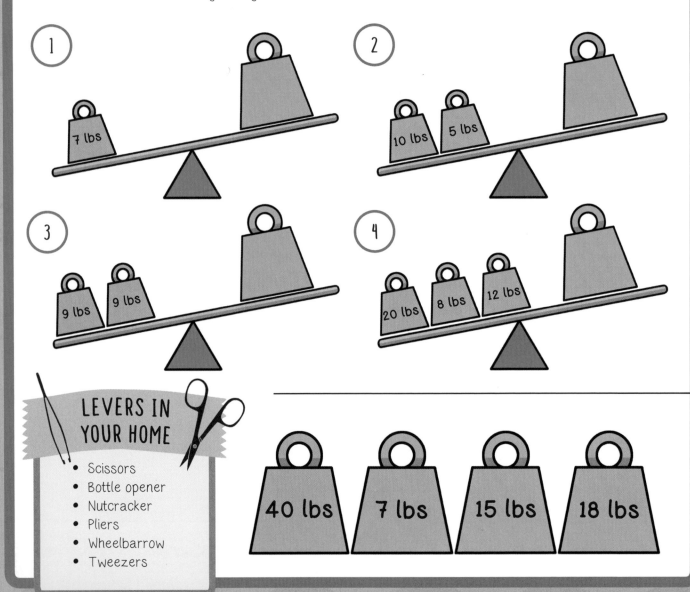

1) 7 lbs

2) 10 lbs 5 lbs

3) 9 lbs 9 lbs

4) 20 lbs 8 lbs 12 lbs

LEVERS IN YOUR HOME

- Scissors
- Bottle opener
- Nutcracker
- Pliers
- Wheelbarrow
- Tweezers

40 lbs   7 lbs   15 lbs   18 lbs

CHECK THE ANSWERS AT THE BACK OF THE BOOK!

Forward motion

Friction is the resistance of motion when one object rubs against another.

Friction resists sliding

The first known use of the wheel was in ancient Mesopotamia, 3,500 B.C., where potters used discs to spin clay to make their pots.

ACTIVITY

We use wheels everywhere today. How many wheels can you see? Count them and then color the busy scene.

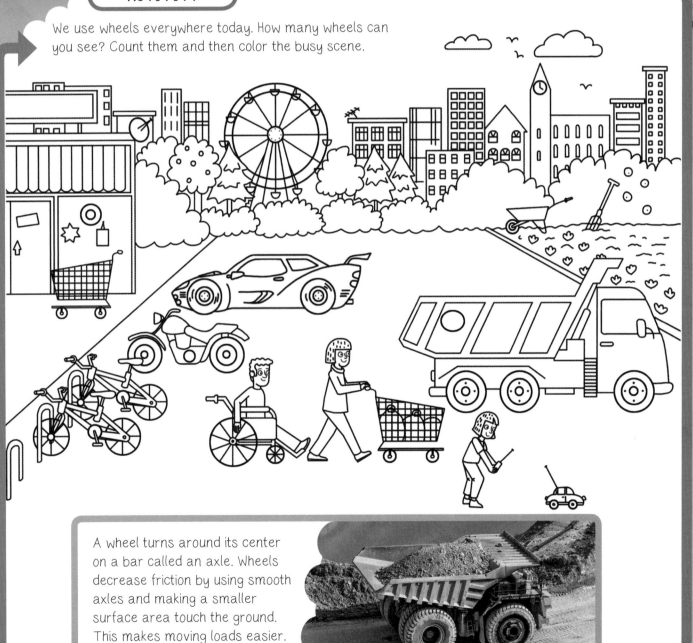

A wheel turns around its center on a bar called an axle. Wheels decrease friction by using smooth axles and making a smaller surface area touch the ground. This makes moving loads easier.

CHECK THE ANSWERS AT THE BACK OF THE BOOK!

TURNING AND PULLING POWER

Gears and pulleys are really useful mechanisms to make machines move smoothly or to lift heavy weights. Gears are like wheels with teeth-shaped points around their edges. Gears interlock to change the turning direction, strength, and speed of a force. Cars and bikes use gears to help them climb steep hills.

ACTIVITY

When two gears meet, the first gear forces the second gear in the opposite direction. The direction of the first three gears is shown with arrows in this picture. Draw in more arrows to show the direction of force for the rest of the gears in the gear train.

CHECK THE ANSWERS AT THE BACK OF THE BOOK!

PULLEYS

A pulley is a wheel with a grooved slot around its edge for a rope or a cable. Lots of pulleys work together to reduce the force needed to lift heavy objects. Adding pulleys multiplies the force and makes the lifting work easier. Cranes, elevators, and drawbridges all use pulley mechanisms.

ACTIVITY

Fill in the missing rope to connect these pulleys, and then draw something heavy for them to lift.

MAN-MADE MATERIALS

Before we can build or design something new, it is important to choose the right materials for the job. Some natural materials like wood, stone, and silk are ready to use just as they are. Other materials need to be manufactured. These are called man-made materials.

STEPHANIE KWOLEK

In 1965, an American chemist named Stephanie Kwolek invented a material called Kevlar. The special fiber is five times stronger than steel and is used in bulletproof vests, body armor, bicycle tires, and frying pans.

ACTIVITY

What am I? Unscramble the letters to name each man-made material.

1

I am light and easy to bend.
I am made from oil.

TICPSAL

....

2

I am transparent.
I am made by melting sand.

SALSG

....

3

I am very hard.
I am mostly made from iron.

SELET

....

4

I am easy to rip.
I am made from wood.

PERAP

....

5

I can hold liquid.
I am made from baked clay.

MECCARI

....

Composite materials combine or mix two or more different materials. Bulletproof glass is a composite. It contains a mix of glass and plastic that makes it extra strong and shatterproof.

CHECK THE ANSWERS AT THE BACK OF THE BOOK!

FANTASTIC PLASTIC

From colorful toys to modern mobile devices, plastic is all around us. It is a versatile material that can be produced in many forms. Plastic can be soft or hard, strong or lightweight, and durable or designed for single use.

Molecules are groups of atoms in a substance that are held together by chemical bonds. Polymers are long chains of molecules containing carbon (C), hydrogen (H), and sometimes other types of atoms. Plastics are made mainly from the molecules found in crude oil (gasoline) and coal. They are a type of polymer.

ACTIVITY

These are drawings of the molecules in plastic polymer chains. Look for the repeating patterns, and then complete each chain. Can you draw the molecules, add the labels, and color the chains in?

POLYETHYLENE

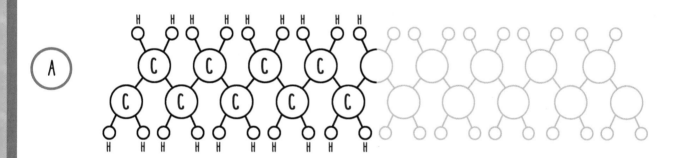

A

POLYPROPYLENE

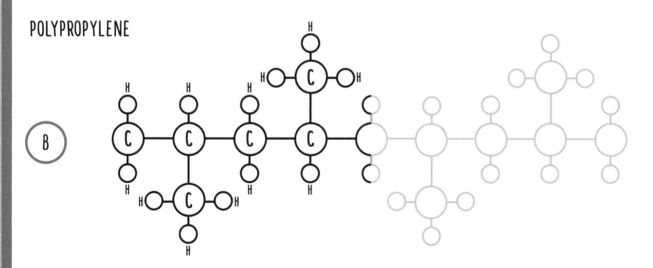

B

SOLID CERAMICS

To transform some materials into useful objects, you need heat to melt or harden the material. Clay and glass are both ceramic materials. When clay, which is fine particles of rock or earth, is heated, it becomes hard and waterproof. The water in it evaporates (disappears as it becomes a gas), and the clay particles harden and bond together.

Glass is made from a chemical compound called silica, which is found in sand. When it's heated, silica becomes runny and can be blown into different shapes as it cools.

ACTIVITY

Color in the shapes by matching the colored dots to complete this beautiful stained-glass window.

FLEXIBLE TEXTILES

Thousands of years ago, our ancestors learned how to sew animal skins together to make clothes to keep them warm. Now we can make clothes and other textiles (fabrics) from many different natural or synthetic (man-made) substances, such as cotton, silk, wool, nylon, and polyester.

A textile can be made from natural or man-made fibers. The fibers are spun into yarns (threads), which are then woven or knitted together. Textiles are used for all kinds of items, such as clothes, sails, medical bandages, carpets, backpacks, and seat belts.

ACTIVITY

Did you know that quilting was an early form of recycling? It used scraps of old material to make new blankets and clothes. Find these patterns in the quilt design below.

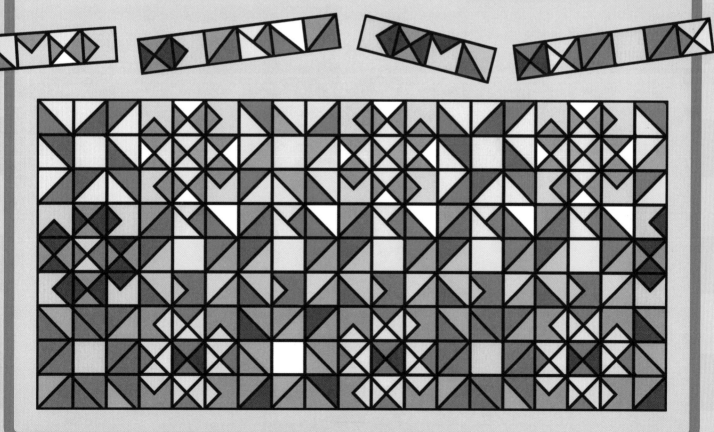

MIGHTY METALS

Metals are natural materials found in rocks called ores. They have to be extracted from the ores before we can use them. The ore is heated to a very high temperature until it melts so that the molten (liquid) metal can be separated out.

FRIEDRICH MOHS

German geologist Friedrich Mohs created the scale of hardness for metals. He graded each metal on a scale of 1 to 10 by determining which materials could scratch each metal and which materials each metal could scratch. The higher the number, the harder the metal.

PROPERTIES OF METALS

Malleability: can bend in all directions without cracking
Conductivity: conducts heat or electrical energy
Durability: can withstand wear, especially weathering
Hardness: able to resist wear, scratching, and indentation
Ductility: able to bend, usually by stretching lengthwise

ACTIVITY

Look at these metal objects. Why is the metal right for the purpose of the object? List one or two properties (explained above) of each metal that make it right for its job.

Zinc battery

....
....
....

Iron frying pan

....
....
....

Gold ring

....
....
....

Tin can

....
....
....

CHECK THE ANSWERS AT THE BACK OF THE BOOK!

When two metals are mixed together or added to other substances like plastic or ceramics, they make a new material called an alloy. Alloys combine the best characteristics of the materials mixed together.

METAL	HARDNESS	PURE/ALLOY	MIX OF METALS
Lead	1.5	Pure	
Zinc	2.5	Pure	
Gold	2.5 to 3	Pure	
Silver	2.5 to 3	Pure	
Brass	3	Alloy	Copper and Zinc
Bronze	3	Alloy	Copper and Tin
Copper	3	Pure	
Nickel	4	Pure	
Platinum	4 to 4.5	Pure	
Steel	4 to 4.5	Alloy	Iron plus another element. There are many types of steel, depending on the other elements mixed with the iron.
Titanium	6	Pure	

ACTIVITY

Be a metallurgist! Test your knowledge of metals by taking this short quiz! Use the table above to help you.

Metallurgists study metals and their properties. They are always trying to create new alloys.

A. I'm an alloy, harder than zinc but softer than nickel, and I am used as a medal for coming in 3rd place.

B. If I am mixed with zinc, I make brass. What am I?

C. I am not the hardest metal in the table, but I'm an alloy used to construct cars, buildings, and more.

D. I'm used to make jewelry and awards for hit records, and I'm harder than gold and silver, but softer than titanium.

E. I am the softest metal in the table, but hard enough to make your pencil scribble and draw.

CHECK THE ANSWERS AT THE BACK OF THE BOOK!

PAPER PRODUCTION

Before humans learned how to mass-produce paper, people carved their writing and pictures onto clay tablets or wrote on papyrus (a type of early paper made from reeds) and animal skins.

1. Trees are fell(e) (cut down) and cu into logs.

2. The logs are cut up into small wood chips.

3. Water is added to the wood chips, and the mixture is pulped (mashed up).

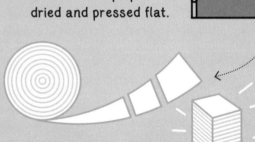

4. The wood pulp is dried and pressed flat.

5. These large, flat sheets are cut into the paper sheets we use every day.

ACTIVITY

Paper can be strong enough to make 3-D packaging. Look at this triangular box. Which letters on the box match up to the numbers on the flat sheet of paper?

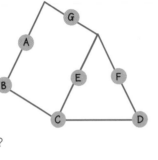

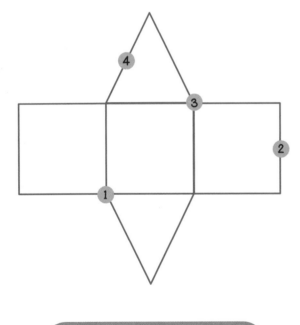

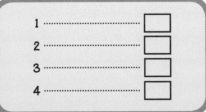

1	☐
2	☐
3	☐
4	☐

CHECK THE ANSWERS AT THE BACK OF THE BOOK!

THE PRINTING PRESS

The invention of Johannes Gutenberg's printing press in the fifteenth century revolutionized technology and learning. Thousands of years ago, only priests, scribes, and nobles could read. Once books could be printed on paper on a large scale, more people learned how to read, creating a growing need for information.

ACTIVITY

Early printing presses used movable wooden letters. They had to be carved back to front so that when they were pressed on the paper, they printed the right way.

Choose either the letters that make up your name or a word of your choice, and copy them here. Use a mirror to read your word!

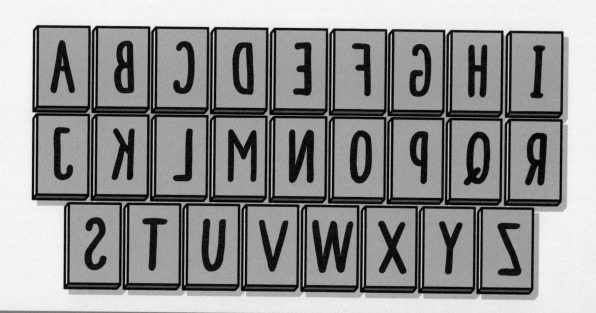

FARM TECHNOLOGY

Technology creates systems to help sow, water, gather, and store crops. Farm technology also uses systems to feed, house, and care for livestock and methods for gathering animal produce, like milk, eggs, and wool.

The farmer needs to make sure all his crops are being watered before he returns to the barn. Follow a route along the water irrigation channels, passing as many fields as possible. Which crops are being watered? Unscramble the letters to find out.

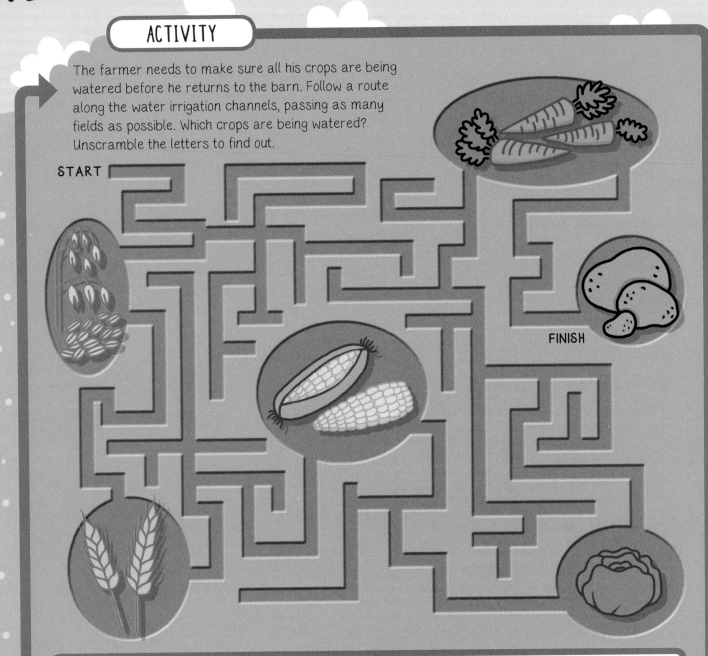

START

FINISH

1. TASO _ _ _ _

2. THEAW _ _ _ _ _

3. NORC _ _ _ _

4. CUTELET _ _ _ _ _ _ _

5. TASCROR _ _ _ _ _ _ _

6. SOPETAOT _ _ _ _ _ _ _ _

CHECK THE ANSWERS AT THE BACK OF THE BOOK!

Agricultural technologists design and build new machines like combine harvesters. They modify (change) crops so the crops have built-in protection from pests and diseases. They also design systems for growing and watering plants without soil.

DID YOU KNOW?

As long as a plant is given water and minerals and its roots are supported, it can grow in containers without soil. This way of growing plants is known as hydroponics.

ACTIVITY

A combine harvester is a machine that combines three harvesting operations—reaping (cutting), threshing (loosening), and winnowing (separating the grain from the crop).

Look at these two pictures. Can you spot five differences between them?

CHECK THE ANSWERS AT THE BACK OF THE BOOK!

ENGINE POWER

Engines are used in all sorts of machines, from cars and motorboats to lawnmowers and aircrafts. They use fuel, like gasoline or diesel. When fuel is heated up by burning or exploding, the energy in it is released. This drives the mechanics of the engine.

In a gasoline engine, used in most cars, a mixture of air and gas is pushed into a hollow cylinder where a spark from a spark plug makes it explode. The force of the explosion pushes a piston down inside the cylinder, which moves a series of gears on a metal shaft. The gears then turn the wheels.

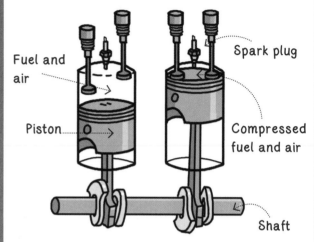

Fuel and air

Spark plug

Piston

Compressed fuel and air

Shaft

ACTIVITY

Oh, no! All of the lawnmowers except one have run out of fuel. Which lawnmower has managed to finish cutting the grass?

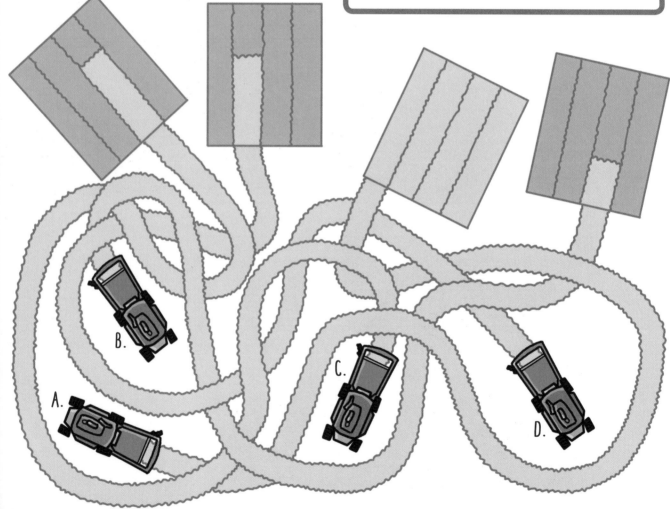

CHECK THE ANSWERS AT THE BACK OF THE BOOK!

These three cars are all going on a road trip to the same destination that is 600 miles (965 kilometers) away. Car A travels at 50 mph (80 kmph), Car B travels at 60 mph (96 kmph) and Car C goes down the country roads at 40 mph (64 kmph). How long, rounded to the nearest hour, does it take each car to reach the destination?

CLUE

Divide the total number of miles by each car's speed.

1

CAR A TAKES _____ HOURS.

2

CAR B TAKES _____ HOURS.

3

CAR C TAKES _____ HOURS.

The gases that come from burning fuel are harmful to the environment. Electric cars don't burn fuel; they use batteries. Scientists have come up with a type of clean technology to replace electric batteries that they hope all cars will use in the future. Instead of a battery, the car uses a hydrogen fuel cell. This power source only produces water and heat, which do not pollute the environment.

CHECK THE ANSWERS AT THE BACK OF THE BOOK!

WATER MOVEMENT

Unless water is contained, it will flow in any direction. To control the movement of water, you need a pump.

HOW DOES A PUMP WORK?

Water will always flow from an area of high air pressure to an area of low air pressure. When you push down a pump, a piston is pressed down into a chamber. This increases the air pressure on the water below, causing the air pressure in the chamber to become lower. As the pump moves up again, the water below is drawn upward toward the area of low air pressure above.

ACTIVITY

A farmer needs to pump water from the river to his fields to water his crops. Follow the pipe shapes through the grid to carry the water to the crops. Your path must follow the order of the four pipe shapes at the top of the grid. You can move up, down, left, and right but not diagonally.

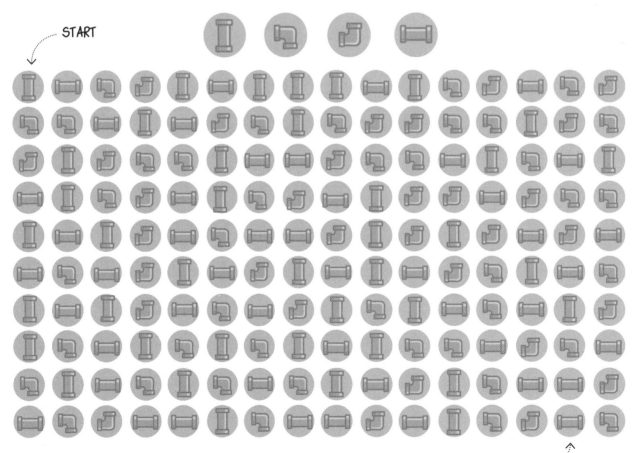

CHECK THE ANSWERS AT THE BACK OF THE BOOK!

BOBBING BUOYANCY

When you put an object in water, gravity pulls it down and displaces (or moves) some of the water. This causes the water beneath the object to push upward. An object is buoyant (will float) if its weight (or density) is equal to or less than the weight of the water pushing up on it.

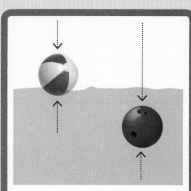

A beach ball takes up the same space as a bowling ball of the same size, so they have the same volume. But the beach ball will float because its volume is mostly air, whereas the bowling ball will sink because it is solid (its mass is denser).

ACTIVITY

Look at this ocean scene. Can you find the five objects that have sunk? Color the picture, and then draw something that will float on the ocean surface.

Why does a huge cargo ship made of metal float, while a small metal coin sinks? The cargo ship is able to remain lighter than the amount of water that it moves because it is not a completely solid object like a small coin. It has empty spaces inside, so its overall density is less than the density of the displaced water pushing back up on the ship.

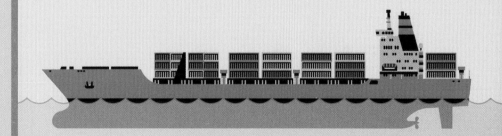

FEARLESS FLIGHT

Humans have always longed to fly like birds, but it wasn't until the beginning of the twentieth century that the Wright brothers built and flew the world's first powered airplane.

ACTIVITY

Up, up, and away! Can you spot ten differences between these amazing flying scenes?

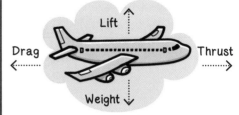

There are four major forces at work when a plane takes off and flies—THRUST, DRAG, LIFT, and WEIGHT.

THRUST   The force made by the engines of an aircraft to make it move forward

DRAG   The force that pulls on the aircraft as it moves through the air

LIFT   The force that keeps the aircraft in the air

WEIGHT   The force of gravity that pulls everything toward Earth

For a plane to take off, there must be more lift than weight and more thrust than drag.

CHECK THE ANSWERS AT THE BACK OF THE BOOK!

A drone is an aircraft without a pilot. It is also known as a UAV (unmanned arial vehicle). It is either controlled by computers inside it (autopilot), or it is under the remote control of a pilot on the ground.

DID YOU KNOW?

A plane has specially shaped wings called airfoils that help increase lift. Airfoils have been inspired by nature. Their design is based on the shape, texture, and movement of humpback whales.

ACTIVITY

Help the pilot navigate this plane through the clouds to land safely at the airport. Move one square at a time, and follow the direction of each arrow to find the right flight path. How many minutes did it take you to land the plane? Time yourself.

It took _____ minutes to land the plane.

RUNWAY

CHECK THE ANSWERS AT THE BACK OF THE BOOK!

BIOTECHNOLOGY

Scientists use microscopes to magnify objects, such as microbes and bacteria, so they can study them in more detail.

Biotechnology is a type of technology that uses living organisms to make new products to improve life and the health of our planet. It is not new technology—we've been using it for centuries to cook, grow plants, breed animals, and make medicine.

ACTIVITY

Use your observation skills like a biotech expert! Study these microscope views of different microbes. Count up all the different colored strands in each dish. The first one has been done for you.

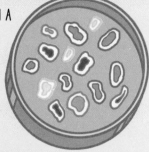
DISH A

There are:

<u>6</u> blue strands   <u>2</u> green strands

<u>4</u> red strands   <u>3</u> yellow strands

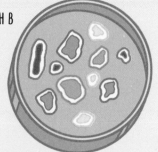
DISH B

There are:

..... blue strands   ..... green strands

..... red strands   ..... yellow strands

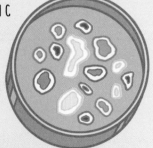
DISH C

There are:

..... blue strands   ..... green strands

..... red strands   ..... yellow strands

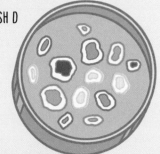
DISH D

There are:

..... blue strands   ..... green strands

..... red strands   ..... yellow strands

The use of microbes, tiny living organisms, is an example of biotechnology in action. The yeast we use in bread is a microbe. When it is added to flour, it produces carbon dioxide gas as it feeds off the sugars in the flour. This gas makes the bread rise.

CHECK THE ANSWERS AT THE BACK OF THE BOOK!

GENETIC ENGINEERING

Every living thing is made up of cells. The cells contain molecules called deoxyribonucleic acid (DNA). This DNA holds the instructions (the genes) telling our bodies how to function and develop. It is like a computer program that tells each cell how to do its job. Under a microscope, the DNA molecule looks like a twisted ladder. This shape is called a double helix.

DID YOU KNOW?

DNA is a long, thin molecule that is made up of four smaller molecules called base pairs—adenine (A), thymine (T), cytosine (C), and guanine (G). DNA molecules are made up of thousands of these pairs, like puzzle pieces.

ACTIVITY

Can you complete the double helix? Match the letters up to the right numbers, and put the pieces of this DNA molecule back together again.

A –
B –
C –
D –

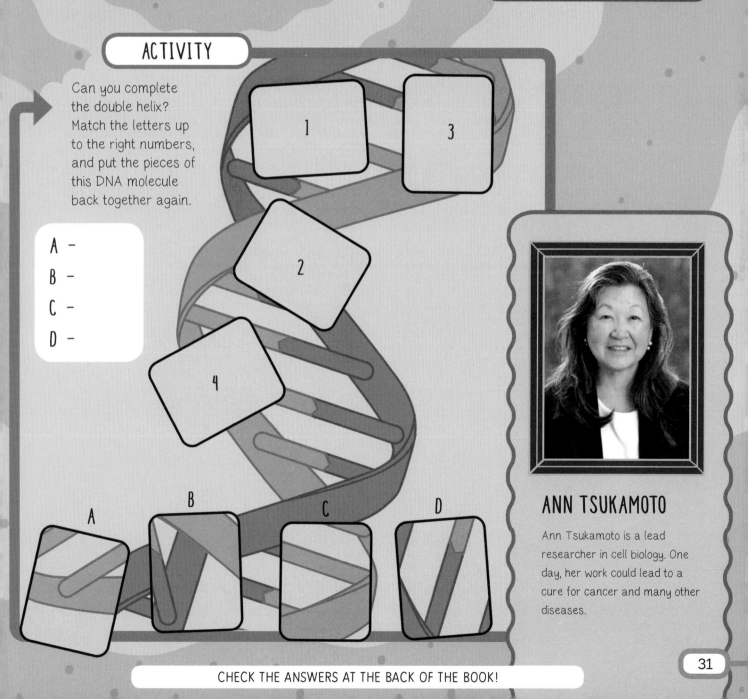

ANN TSUKAMOTO

Ann Tsukamoto is a lead researcher in cell biology. One day, her work could lead to a cure for cancer and many other diseases.

31

MEDICAL TECHNOLOGY

A medical technologist uses his/her knowledge to build machines, products, and systems that can diagnose or treat diseases, illnesses, or injuries.

DA VINCI SURGERY

The da Vinci Surgical System combines the skill of doctors with the latest robotics technology. Doctors use da Vinci's magnified 3-D, high-definition vision system along with tiny instruments to complete complicated surgery.
The da Vinci Robot can bend and rotate more than a human hand. Surgeons are able to operate with much more precision and control than ever before, which makes the surgery easier for the patient.

ACTIVITY

The doctor below is using the da Vinci system to carry out heart surgery. The high tech machinery allows the doctor to see the heart magnified and in 3-D. Look at this image of a heart, and then copy it carefully into the magnified grid.

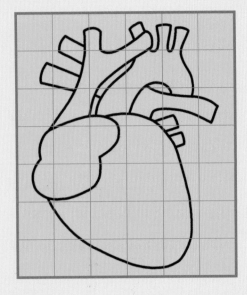

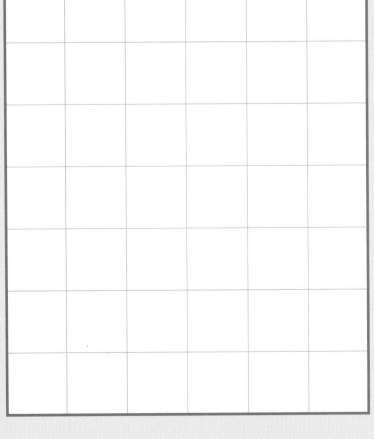

If someone is missing a body part because of illness or an accident, medical technology can often provide a man-made implant called a prosthesis. The prosthesis can do the job of the injured or missing part. When combined with electronic technologies, these prosthetic limbs are even more controllable. These amazing medical inventions have changed the way people can be treated and how they can live.

ACTIVITY

Here is amazing medical technology in action!
Connect the dots to find out what it is.

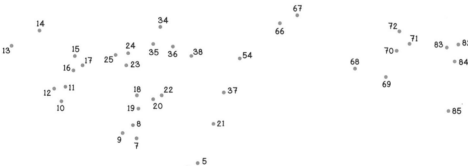

SPARKING ELECTRICITY

Most of our technological gadgets wouldn't work without electricity. Electricity is a force produced by the flow of electrons in an electric current. Electricity only flows in a complete loop or circuit. If you break the circuit, the flow will stop. A circuit always needs a power source to get the electrons flowing around it.

ACTIVITY

Look at the electric circuit in the green panel. Use it to help you decide which of the circuits below will also work. Color each bulb that will light.

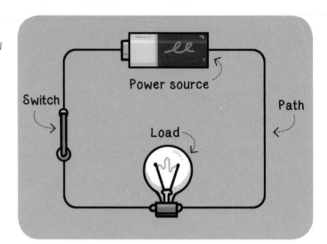

A

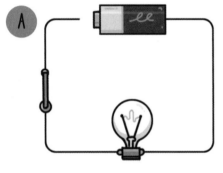

B

C

D

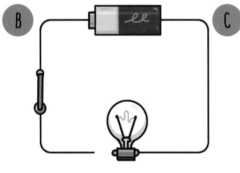

E

F

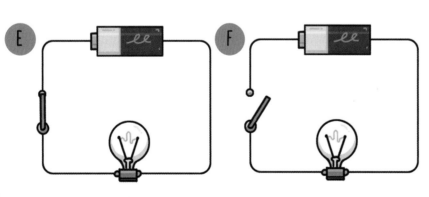

An atom contains particles called electrons and protons. The electrons carry a negative charge and the protons carry a positive charge. These charged particles exert a force on other charged particles. The flow (movement) of these charged particles is electricity. Electrons always flow from negative to positive.

CHECK THE ANSWERS AT THE BACK OF THE BOOK!

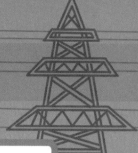

The electricity we use every day is made in a power station and is carried along pylons (cables) to our homes, schools, hospitals, and offices. The current is produced by the movement of a metal coil as it rotates inside a strong magnetic field produced by powerful magnets.

ACTIVITY

Did you know that electricity flows through some substances like metals (conductors), and not through others like wood (insulators)? Are the following substances conductors or insulators?
Be a techie and do some research, or make a guess based on your experience.
Write "conductor" or "insulator" in the white boxes below.

1. WATER   2. GLASS   3. PLASTIC   4. COPPER

5. GOLD   6. CERAMIC   7. PAPER   8. SILVER

9. RUBBER   10. ALUMINUM

1		6	
2		7	
3		8	
4		9	
5		10	

DID YOU KNOW?

Touch screens are just another completed circuit. Your body can conduct electricity. When you press a touch-sensitive screen with your finger, you are completing a circuit. This makes electricity flow and completes your selected action.

CHECK THE ANSWERS AT THE BACK OF THE BOOK!

MAGNETS AND MOTORS

We use motors in many things from household gadgets to medical devices like MRI scanners and from CERN's Large Hadron Collider to trains. To build a motor, you need to combine the force of electricity with that of magnets to make an electromagnet.

A magnet has a north and a south pole. The magnetic force flows from the north to the south pole, creating an area around the magnet called a magnetic field. The north and south poles pull toward each other, while two like poles (north–north or south–south) push away from each other.

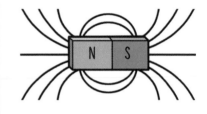

ACTIVITY

Draw in direction arrows to show whether these magnets are attracting or repelling (pushing away) each other. The first one has been done for you.

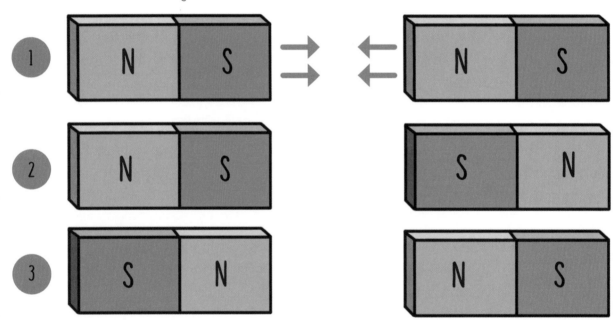

ELECTRIC MOTOR

An electric motor uses a wire loop placed between two magnets. When an electric current runs through the wire, it creates a magnetic field around it. The direction of the current is constantly switched to reverse the magnetic field around the loop. The constant pulling and pushing of magnetic forces keep the wire loop spinning and give the motor its turning power.

Electric Motor

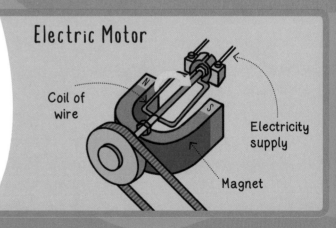

Coil of wire

Electricity supply

Magnet

CHECK THE ANSWERS AT THE BACK OF THE BOOK!

MAKING IT BIGGER

A microscope uses special glass lenses to make very small things look thousands of times bigger. A telescope uses special glass lenses to see things that are far away. The lenses used in microscopes and telescopes bend the light waves traveling through them to magnify the objects being looked at.

ACTIVITY

Use the clues to figure out what the scientists are looking at through these microscope and telescope lenses.

MICROSCOPE

1
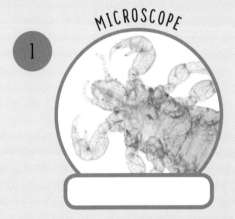

I live in hair, and I make you itch!

TELESCOPE

2

I was built as the final resting place for kings by the longest river in the world.

TELESCOPE

3
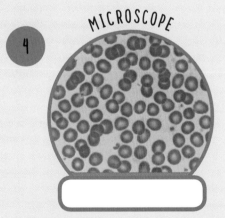

I am a large planet with rings made of chunks of ice and rock.

MICROSCOPE

4

I am part of the liquid substance that flows through your body.

CHECK THE ANSWERS AT THE BACK OF THE BOOK!

FROM ANALOG TO DIGITAL

Any device or gadget that we use to communicate with, or carry information on, needs to have a way of sending, receiving, storing, and using this information. The information is encoded and sent as either an analog or a digital electrical signal from a transmitter to a receiver. The signal is then decoded so that you can hear the voice of someone on the phone or see the information on your screen.

ACTIVITY

Clocks and watches work using either analog or digital technology. Look at the analog clocks at the top, and then write the correct times on the digital clocks underneath. The first one has been done for you.

ANALOG CLOCKS

DIGITAL CLOCKS

An analog signal is a continuous electrical signal. It loses its quality over distance. A digital signal is a stronger, noncontinuous electrical signal. It is a series of electric pulses, which are either ON or OFF.

To read digital signals, a device changes them into a digital form using the digits 1 (ON) and 0 (OFF). This code, called binary code, is then translated into words, sounds, and images that we can understand.

ACTIVITY

Put this list in order from the biggest to the smallest.

KILOBYTE

GIGABYTE

NIBBLE

BIT

TERABYTE

BYTE

MEGABYTE

1. ....

2. ....

3. ....

4. ....

5. ....

6. ....

7. ....

BITS AND BYTES

Each 1 and 0 in the binary code is called a bit.

A nibble is 4 bits (or half a byte).
A byte is 8 bits.
A kilobyte (KB) is 1,000 bytes.
A megabyte (MB) is 1,000 kilobytes.
A gigabyte (GB) is 1,000 megabytes.
A terabyte (TB) is 1,000 gigabytes.

CHECK THE ANSWERS AT THE BACK OF THE BOOK!

COOL COMPUTERS

A computer is an electronic machine that can do lots of different jobs. It stores information (data) and processes (organizes) it. You can access and add information, make changes, or do calculations.

Information or data put into a computer is called input.
The information that we access is called output.
The stored information in the computer is called memory.

The physical parts of a computer that do the work, like the mouse and keyboard, are called hardware.
They follow the instructions from the software programs installed on the computer.

ACTIVITY

Which of these devices are "input" and which are "output"? Draw a line to show each device's job. Draw a dotted line for input and a straight line for output.

KEYBOARD

MONITOR SCREEN

MOUSE

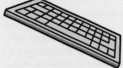

SPEAKER

MICROPHONE

PRINTER

ADA LOVELACE

Ada Lovelace was a gifted mathematician. She wrote instructions for the first computer program in the mid-1800s, which was started by her mentor, Charles Babbage.

CHECK THE ANSWERS AT THE BACK OF THE BOOK!

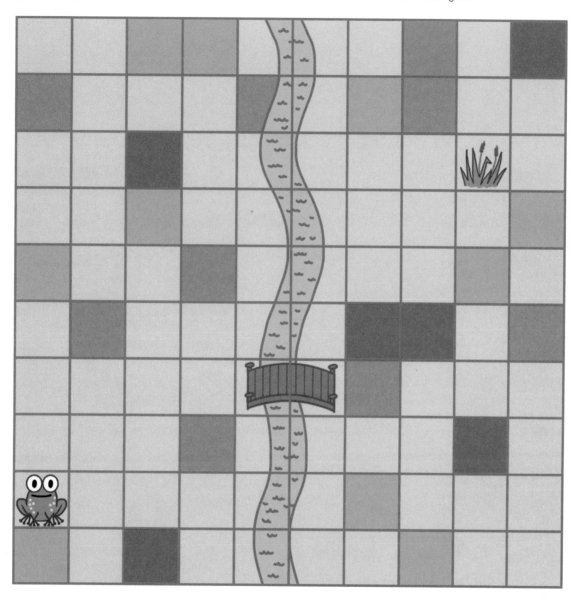

ACTIVITY

Computer software works on logical statements called commands. Complete the logic statements to get the frog over the river. The first two statements have been done for you.

Start on the square that the frog is in.

Move 2 blocks to the right of the square the frog is in.

Move 4 blocks up toward the top of the grid.

Move _ block to the right toward the river.

Move _ blocks down to step onto the bridge.

Move _ blocks to the right to cross the bridge.

Move _ blocks up toward the top of the grid.

Move _ blocks to the right to reach the reeds.

AWESOME APPS

Applications or "apps" are another type of software. An app uses the device's system software to give its instructions to the computer. When you buy an app, it needs to be able to work with your system software.

ACTIVITY

Many apps make day-to-day life easier. What is a task or function you wish could be easier in your day? Do you need reminders to feed your dog or to do your homework? Design an app for that! Describe your app here and say what it would do, who would use it, and what kind of device you are designing it for. Draw your app icon, and give it an awesome name.

ACTIVITY

Your new cell phone has apps for the following things—maps, messages, weather forecast, photo gallery, music, homework planner, calculator, and a game. Design a new app icon for each category.

TYPES OF APPS

- Games
- Puzzles
- Stories
- Maps
- Math practice
- Music
- Drawing
- Recipes
- Places to go out
- Calendar
- Fitness tracker
- Health tracker
- Messaging

COMPUTER GRAPHICS

To enjoy your computer games, other programs, and apps to their fullest, your screen resolution (quality) needs to be high. Luckily, technology is at hand! The quality of your picture depends on the size of something called a pixel.

The smaller the size of each pixel, the better the quality of the computer graphics. As technology has improved, more pixels are used to make up a picture. This means the picture becomes sharper. Unless you zoom in, you can't see the pixels.

ACTIVITY

Look at this colorful picture. Each square on the grid is a pixel, making up a pixelated picture of a rocket. The rocket is headed to Saturn. Draw a pixelated picture of the planet Saturn in the next grid.

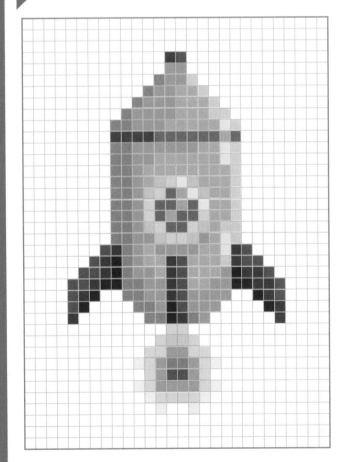

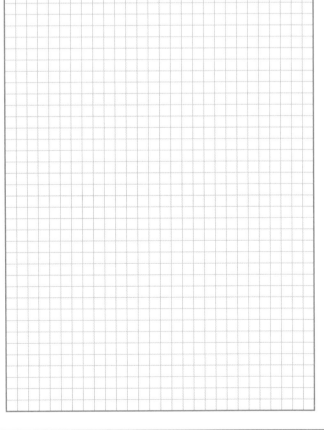

Computer graphics can create all sorts of visual effects using pixels. Color each square the same color as the dot on the square. Watch an amazing 3-D image pop out.

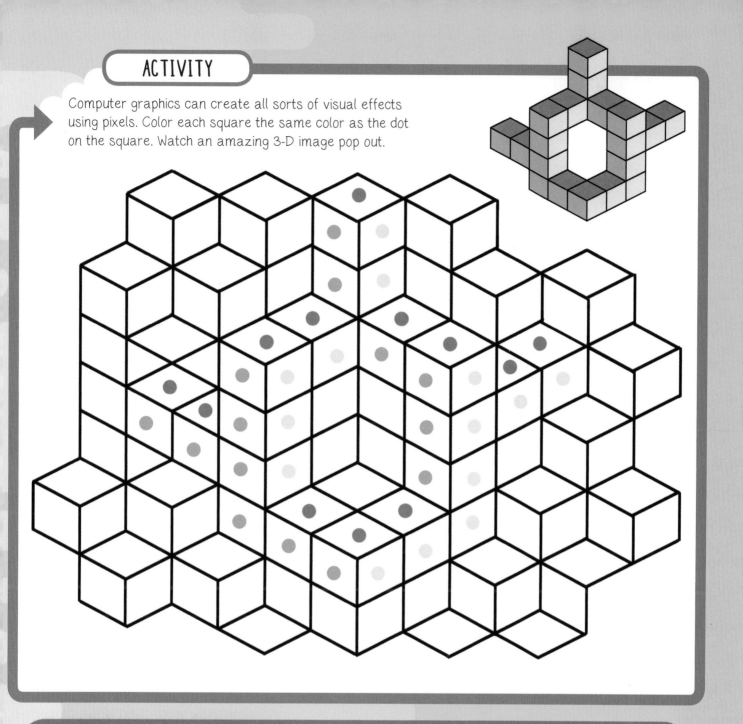

Movies and computer games make use of the newest graphic techniques to produce the best visual effects. Using a technology called CGI (computer-generated imagery), amazing 3-D images can be made that look as realistic as actual movie footage.

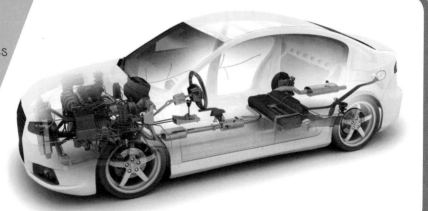

PHONE A FRIEND

Many of us have a cell phone, but these pocket-size devices have only been around for the last 30 years or so. Before then, people used the telephone to speak to friends and family who were far away. Telephones work by turning sounds into electrical signals and sending them down a wire.

Cell phones send and receive calls using microwaves. The information doesn't need to travel along wires or cables. It is sent as a digital signal to the nearest cell phone tower.

ALEXANDER GRAHAM BELL

In 1876, Alexander Graham Bell became the first to patent (legally protect) his invention of the telephone, although there were others not far behind him.

Cell phone towers help pick up and send messages. If you are not near a tower, or you are outside of the area of its signal coverage, your phone may not be able to pick up a signal, and you won't be able to make or receive a call.

Grace is on the way to her friend Daisy's house. She is running late and needs to phone her friend to let her know. Which route should Grace take to get the best signal coverage while she is walking?

First, put a check next to each location with WiFi coverage (a signal). Next, draw her route for the best connection.

By the pond in the park

The café on Main Street

Inside the candy store

Outside the supermarket

By the mailbox on the corner of Cross Road

Outside the train station

WIRELESS TECHNOLOGY

Although we can't see them, the air is full of waves—light waves, radio waves, microwaves, and X-rays. Waves release energy in the form of electricity and magnetism as they travel. Together they are known as electromagnetic waves and form part of an electromagnetic spectrum. The different types of waves have different wavelengths and different frequencies.

Phones, TVs, radios, X-rays, and microwaves use signals made up of electromagnetic waves to do their jobs. Radio waves have the longest wavelength and gamma rays have the shortest. The shorter the wavelength, the more frequency it has—and the more energy.

ACTIVITY

There are seven different types of waves in the electromagnetic spectrum. Can you find each type in the word search grid?

RADIO WAVES
MICROWAVES
INFRARED
VISIBLE LIGHT
ULTRAVIOLET
X-RAYS
GAMMA RAYS

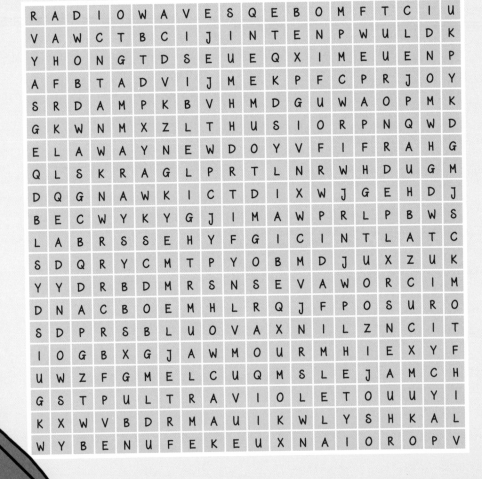

CHECK THE ANSWERS AT THE BACK OF THE BOOK!

X-rays are used to take pictures of the dense bones in bodies. Look at these X-rays of animals taken by a veterinarian. Can you tell what animals they are? Which animal has a broken bone?

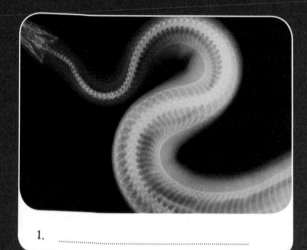

1. _____

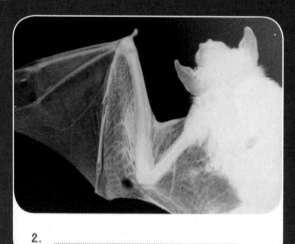

2. _____

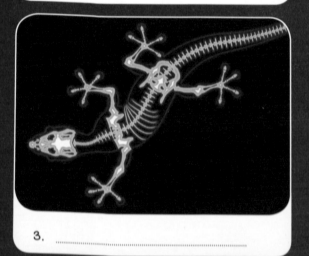

3. _____

4. _____

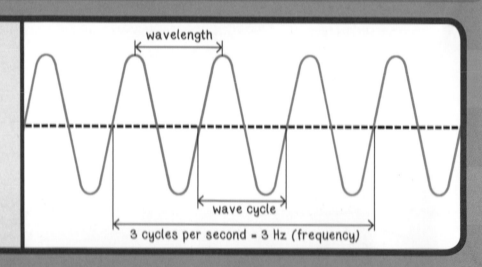

Wavelength is the distance between the peak of one wave to the peak of the next. Frequency is the measure of how often a wave repeats in a second.

wavelength

wave cycle

3 cycles per second = 3 Hz (frequency)

CHECK THE ANSWERS AT THE BACK OF THE BOOK!

INCREDIBLE INTERNET

The Internet is a worldwide network that links electronic devices together. Each device can communicate with other devices, wherever they are in the world, to allow people to chat, send pictures and messages, share information, buy things, and play games.

All the information or data traveling around the Internet is sent in the form of electrical signals via cables or satellite.

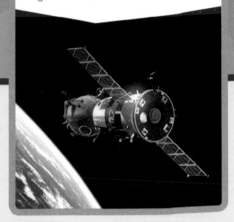

HOW THE INTERNET WORKS

Message (packet)

When someone looks for information on the Internet, that search is a message organized as a "packet" and is sent to a server—a large computer that receives and processes the data being sent. The server then sends back the web page. To do this, the web page is broken down into many "packets." The electronic device receives these packets and reassembles (downloads) them so that the person can view the complete web page on his or her screen.

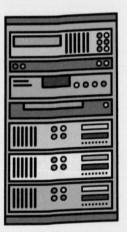

Server

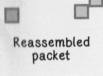

Reassembled packet

Broken down packets

DID YOU KNOW?

Data packets are huge and complex. They take time to reassemble. Buffering allows packets of media files or streamed video to be downloaded while the user is listening to it or watching it.

ACTIVITY

Sometimes not all data loads at once. On the left, there are all of the data packets for a web page picture. Fill in the missing packets in the correct places on the right so that you can see the completed image on your screen.

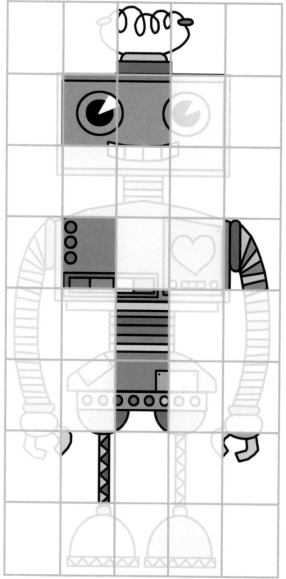

Every electronic device has something called an IP (Internet Protocol) address. Without this address, devices would not be able to send or receive information. The packets would get lost!

HELLO

HELLO

VIRTUAL REALITY

Virtual reality (VR) allows us to experience an artificial world and to participate in that environment. VR technology, such as sophisticated computer-generated graphics and sensory equipment like headsets and gloves, is needed to interact and explore a virtual world.

VR technology can be used to train airline pilots and help surgeons practice difficult procedures and operations. Athletes use VR to assist them with their sports training, and car manufacturers can use it to test car designs.

ACTIVITY

This is a VR challenge set up to train firefighters how to fight a fire. Write three tasks the firefighter will need to practice at this scene. Try to spot the hazards in the picture.

Task 1 ....

Task 2 ....

Task 3 ....

ARTIFICIAL INTELLIGENCE

Artificial intelligence (AI) is the technology used to create computer programs, machines, or robots that can "think," learn, and copy intelligent human behavior.

Scientists have already built robots that look and behave like humans. The robots mimic human behaviors—they can understand simple instructions and even hold conversations. They can move like humans, too. They walk and run, as well as lift and carry objects.

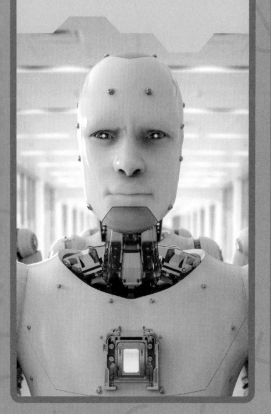

Scientists are using AI to develop smart self-driving cars. These cars will learn to drive in the same way that humans do—through experience—so that they can go out on the roads without a driver.

ACTIVITY

A humanoid robot can be programmed to recognize human expressions. Test your own observation skills, and match the correct mirror image to each face.

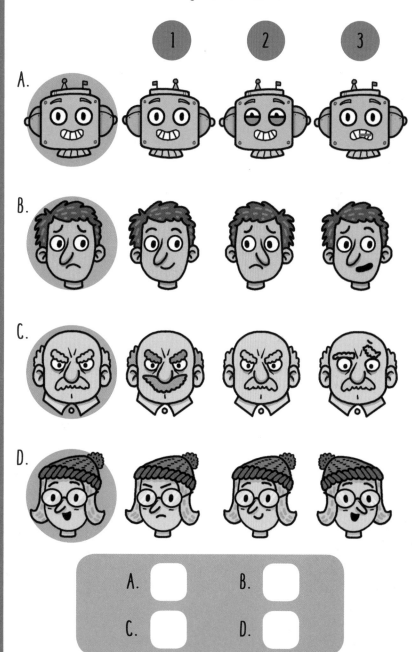

ROBOT REVOLUTION

Robot technology is advancing all the time. Scientists can build and program robots to entertain us, educate us, or help us do many jobs—some of which are too dangerous for us to do.

In the automotive industry, robots perform many tasks like welding and painting. This increases productivity (the speed and quality of the work).

Surveillance robots can go into a danger zone, like an earthquake, to check for survivors and the safety of a building. They can take pictures and record data in difficult-to-reach or dangerous environments, like the bottom of the ocean or a planet in space.

ACTIVITY

You have been asked to design a robot for an elderly person living on his or her own.

List four tasks that an elderly person needs help with in his or her home.

TARGET TASKS

1. ....

2. ....

3. ....

4. ....

Draw the "blueprint" for your robot and give it a name. Make sure that it has all of the movement and communication tools it needs to complete your four target tasks.

GIVE YOUR ROBOT A NAME.

SPACE TECHNOLOGY

Space technology is out of this world! Scientists have developed rockets to get humans into space, telescopes that can take deep-space photographs, and probes that collect data on planets and comets. They build vehicles to explore the moon and Mars and space stations for astronauts to live in and do research.

The International Space Station (ISS) is the largest manned object ever sent into space. It is powered by solar energy and can be seen from Earth moving across the sky at night. It orbits 248 miles (402 kilometers) above Earth and circles Earth every 90 minutes.

ACTIVITY

Design your own space station on Mars! Think about what things you will need—a place to grow plants, a water recycling center, a medical unit, a communications center, a research lab, an energy generator, a vehicle repair workshop, and a docking station.

DID YOU KNOW?

The ISS has its own space worker robot named Dextre. Dextre does outside jobs, like adding new gadgets or parts to the ISS. It is remotely controlled by a technician from inside the ISS.

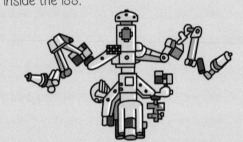

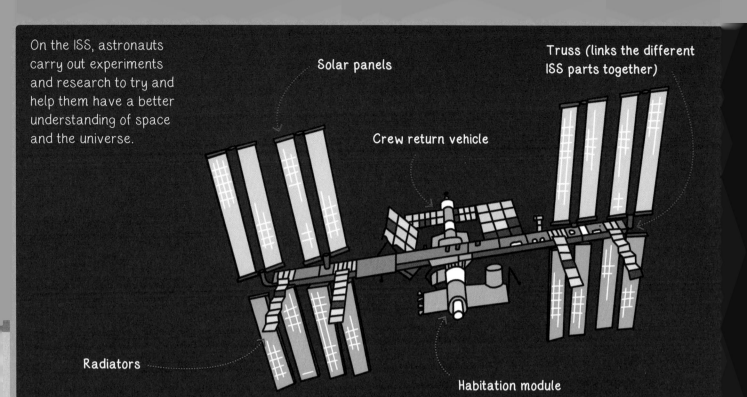

On the ISS, astronauts carry out experiments and research to try and help them have a better understanding of space and the universe.

Solar panels

Truss (links the different ISS parts together)

Crew return vehicle

Radiators

Habitation module

SUPER SPACE SUITS

A space suit is an intelligently designed piece of technology that helps an astronaut survive the extreme conditions in space. The suit allows astronauts to breathe by providing oxygen and taking away the carbon dioxide that is exhaled. It also protects them from flying space debris, extreme temperatures, and the sun's harmful rays.

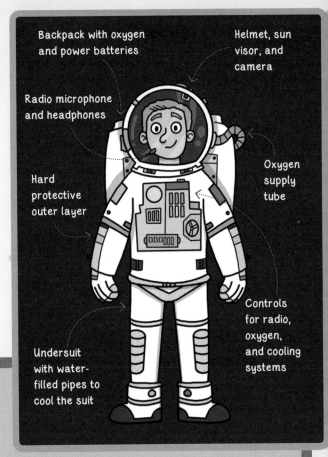

Backpack with oxygen and power batteries

Helmet, sun visor, and camera

Radio microphone and headphones

Hard protective outer layer

Oxygen supply tube

Controls for radio, oxygen, and cooling systems

Undersuit with water-filled pipes to cool the suit

ACTIVITY

An astronaut has taken several pictures on his space walk outside the ISS. He zoomed his lens in close to capture these images. Can you figure out what he saw?

1

2

3

4

CHECK THE ANSWERS AT THE BACK OF THE BOOK!

EXPLORATORY SPACE VEHICLES

Did you know that more than 100 robots armed with high-tech gadgets and instruments have been sent into space to visit and explore planets, moons, comets, and asteroids? They take photos and gather data and samples to help scientists with their space research.

ACTIVITY

This rover will use sensors to find five different rock samples. Can you spot the different rocks in the picture?

Rovers are advanced unmanned vehicles that are dropped onto planets. Once they land, they can roam on a large area of the surface, and collect data and samples.

CHECK THE ANSWERS AT THE BACK OF THE BOOK!

TECHNOLOGY FUTURE

Technology is always moving forward. New gadgets and devices are being invented all the time! Who knows what amazing machines we might have in the future? We are already closer to having driverless cars and smart humanoid robots that can interact with us.

ACTIVITY

Many big scientific, medical, technical, and engineering companies are now working together to create new technologies. The more people share their ideas, knowledge, and skills, the better the machines of the future will be.

You could be the inventor, scientist, engineer, or designer of our future technology! Use this grid paper to design a new gadget that would help people all over the world. How could it work? What could it do?

THE BIG TECHNOLOGY QUIZ

Now it's time to test your technology knowledge! Check the right answers. Look back through the book if you need to check your facts.

1

Which mechanism is used to help machines move smoothly or lift heavy weights?

a) Fulcrum ☐

b) Gears and pulleys ☐

c) Microchip ☐

2

Glass is made by...

a) Polishing stone ☐

b) Mining rock ☐

c) Melting sand ☐

3

If a metal is malleable, it can...

a) Bend in all directions without cracking ☐   b) Withstand weathering ☐   c) Conduct heat ☐

4

When two or more materials are mixed together, they form...

a) An ore ☐

b) An alloy ☐

c) A polymer ☐

5

Who invented the printing press?

a) Mohs ☐

b) Bell ☐

c) Gutenberg ☐

6

If an object is buoyant, it will...

a) Fly ☐

b) Sink ☐

c) Float ☐

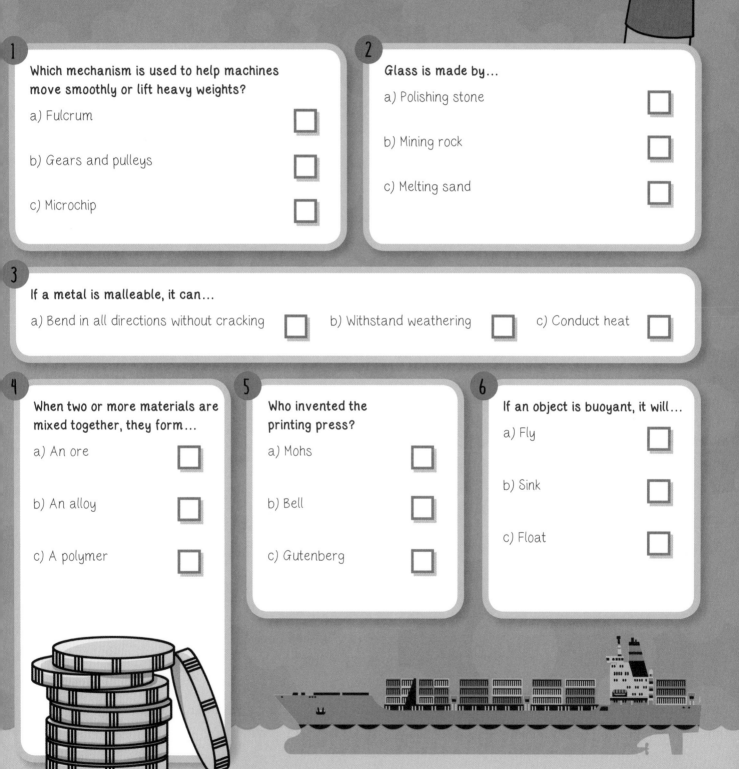

CHECK THE ANSWERS AT THE BACK OF THE BOOK!

7

The four major forces at work when a plane takes off and flies are...

a) Magnetism, drag, electricity, and thrust ☐

b) Thrust, drag, lift, and weight ☐

c) Buoyancy, thrust, heat, and drag ☐

8

Which type of technology uses living organisms to make new products for humans?

a) Biotechnology ☐

b) Plantechnology ☐

c) Meditechnology ☐

9

Magnetic force always flows...

a) From the south pole to the north pole ☐

b) Between the same poles ☐

c) From the north pole to the south pole ☐

10

What is binary code made up of?

a) 1s and 2s ☐   b) 0s and 1s ☐   c) 0s and 5s ☐

11

"Pixel" stands for...

a) Photo Cells ☐

b) Photographic Program ☐

c) Picture Element ☐

12

Which of these waves is not on the electromagnetic spectrum?

a) Radio waves ☐

b) Sound waves ☐

c) Microwaves ☐

ANSWERS

Pages 8-9
IN THE BEGINNING...
1. Pestle and mortar
2. Hoe
3. Hammer
4. Chisel
5. Needle
6. Spear
7. Saw
8. Axe
9. Sickle
10. Arrow

The carpenter is using hammer D.

Pages 10-11
MARVELOUS MACHINES
1. 7 lbs   2. 15 lbs   3. 18 lbs   4. 40 lbs
There are 21 wheels in the picture.

Page 12
TURNING AND PULLING POWER

Page 14
MAN-MADE MATERIALS
1. Plastic   2. Glass   3. Steel   4. Paper   5. Ceramic

Page 17
FLEXIBLE TEXTILES

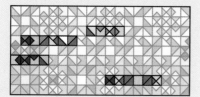

Pages 18-19
MIGHTY METALS

Zinc battery
Conducts electricity
Hard
Plentiful and inexpensive to buy

Iron frying pan
Conducts heat
High melting point
Strong, but can easily rust

Gold ring
Malleable
Ductile
Shiny (good for making jewelry)

Tin can
Durable
Ductile
Resistant to corrosion

A. Bronze   B. Copper   C. Steel
D. Platinum   E. Lead

Page 20
PAPER PRODUCTION
1. B   2. G   3. D   4. E

Pages 22-23
FARM TECHNOLOGY
1. Oats   4. Lettuce
2. Wheat   5. Carrots
3. Corn   6. Potatoes

Pages 24-25
ENGINE POWER
Lawnmower A has finished cutting the grass.
1. Car A takes 12 hours.
2. Car B takes 10 hours.
3. Car C takes 15 hours.

Page 26
WATER MOVEMENT

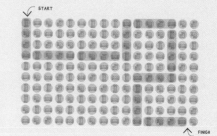

Page 27
BOBBING BUOYANCY

Pages 28-29
FEARLESS FLIGHT

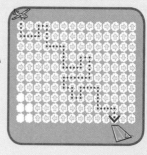

Page 30
BIOTECHNOLOGY

DISH B
3 blue strands   2 green strands
3 red strands   3 yellow strands

DISH C
2 blue strands   4 green strands
5 red strands   4 yellow strands

DISH D

| 4 blue strands | 4 green strands |
| 2 red strands | 4 yellow strands |

Page 31

GENETIC ENGINEERING

A. 4   B. 2   C. 3   D. 1

Page 33

MEDICAL TECHNOLOGY

The image shows a robotic hand holding an egg.

Pages 34-35

SPARKING ELECTRICITY

Circuit E would work.

CONDUCTORS:
Water, copper, gold, silver, aluminum

INSULATORS:
Glass, plastic, ceramic, paper, rubber

Page 36

MAGNETS AND MOTORS

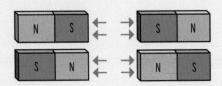

Page 37

MAKING IT BIGGER

1. Head louse   2. Pyramids of Giza
3. Saturn   4. Blood cell

Pages 38-39

FROM ANALOG TO DIGITAL

1. Terabyte   2. Gigabyte   3. Megabyte
4. Kilobyte   5. Byte   6. Nibble   7. Bit

Pages 40-41

COOL COMPUTERS

INPUT: Keyboard, Mouse, Microphone
OUTPUT: Monitor Screen, Printer, Speaker

There are several ways that the frog can get over the river. Here's one set of commands:

Move 2 blocks to the right of the square the frog is in.
Move 4 blocks up toward the top of the grid.
Move 1 block to the right toward the river.
Move 2 blocks down to step onto the bridge.
Move 3 blocks to the right to cross the bridge.
Move 4 blocks up toward the top of the grid.
Move 2 blocks to the right to reach the reeds.

Page 47

PHONE A FRIEND

Page 48-49

WIRELESS TECHNOLOGY

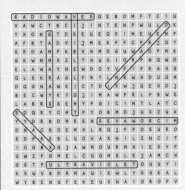

1. Snake
2. Bat
3. Lizard
4. Tortoise

The bat has a broken bone.

Page 53

ARTIFICIAL INTELLIGENCE

A. 1   B. 2   C. 2   D. 3

Page 58

SUPER SPACE SUITS

1. Earth   2. Satellite   3. Dextre   4. Astronaut

Page 59

EXPLORATORY SPACE VEHICLES

Pages 61-62

THE BIG TECHNOLOGY QUIZ

1. b   2. c   3. a   4. b
5. c   6. c   7. b   8. a
9. c   10. b   11. c   12. b